FATHER'S DAY

THE MONSTERS IN THE TRUCK!

BY HELEN MCCARTHY
ILLUSTRATED BY JENNY KELLEY

Published by HelensHouse
Copyright ©2016

ISBN 978-1-4951-8758-2

While reading this book to children,
please put in as many screams and yells and cries
as you can to make this book come alive!

It was Father's Day.

Father's Day is a special day set aside just for Dads.
It is a day to show your Dad how much you love him.

The story begins like this..........

Once upon a time, there were three lovely little girls
named Kylie, Cienna and Caroline.

It was Father's Day.

The three lovely little girls asked their dad,
"What would you like for your special day?
What would you like to do, Dad?"

"Hmmmmmmm," said the Dad.

"I would like to go to the beach for the day!"

So..........the Dad, Mom and three lovely little girls
prepared for the beach.

They packed the cooler and filled it with food and
drinks. They loaded beach chairs, an umbrella,
sunscreen, towels and sand toys!

Everyone climbed into the truck to go to the beach,
safe in their car seats.

Then..........it happened!

The monsters came!

First came the KyKy monster. She was the oldest monster. She yelled loudly, **"I'm going to throw up!"** And..........she did! All over the seat!

Next came the middle monster, Ceena Beena.

She screamed as loudly as she could,
**"I'm sick of being in this truck! Get me out of here!
I'm going to scream until we get there!"**

And..........she did!

Last came the little tiny teeny weeny baby,
the NuNu monster.

She cried in her squeaky baby voice, "**My teeth hurt,
me no like it! Wa wa WAAAAAAA!**"

All the monsters were

        yelling,

               screaming,

                       and crying..........

             until..........

finally,

they arrived at the beach.

As the monsters climbed out of the truck, they transformed back into three lovely little girls.

In their bathing suits, they carried their sand toys and began digging in the sand.

They played in the ocean and collected shells.

They poured water on their Dad's feet to make him comfy in his beach chair.

The Dad sat in his beach chair
relaxing in the warm sun.

He went swimming in the water.

He took the girls in the water on floats.

The Mom was busy getting a picnic lunch
ready on the blanket.

They played in the sand for a while longer, making
sandcastles and roadways for their cars.

They had a wonderful time!

Now it was time for everyone to leave the beach.

The three lovely little girls helped
their Mom and Dad load the truck.

The girls climbed into the truck, safe in their car seats.

Then..........

it happened..........

AGAIN!!!

The Mom tried to give them water and snacks to make
them happy but that didn't work.

The KyKy monster yelled as loudly as she could,
"I'm going to throw up!"

And..........she did! All over the seat!

The Ceena Beena monster screamed,
**"I'm sick of this truck! Get me out of here!
I'm going to scream until we get there!"**

And..........she did!

The tiny teeny weeny baby NuNu monster sobbed and cried, "**My teeth hurt, make the hurt go away!**

Wa wa WAAAAAAA!"

Well, they yelled.......... and screamed..........
and cried..........and they yelled.......... and they
screamed..........and they cried..........

until...........

at last,

they were home.

As they climbed out of the truck, they all turned back
into three lovely little girls.

They helped their Mom and Dad
bring everything into the garage.

The three lovely little girls, the Mom and the Dad took showers and had dinner and then off to bed went the three lovely little girls!

And..........the monsters stayed in the truck.